GHOST STORIES

GHOSTS
IN THE WHITE HOUSE

By Lisa Owings

EPIC

BELLWETHER MEDIA • MINNEAPOLIS, MN

EPIC

EPIC BOOKS are no ordinary books. They burst with intense action, high-speed heroics, and shadows of the unknown. Are you ready for an Epic adventure?

This edition first published in 2017 by Bellwether Media, Inc.

No part of this publication may be reproduced in whole or in part without written permission of the publisher.
For information regarding permission, write to Bellwether Media, Inc., Attention: Permissions Department,
5357 Penn Avenue South, Minneapolis, MN 55419.

Library of Congress Cataloging-in-Publication Data

Names: Owings, Lisa, author.
Title: Ghosts in the White House / by Lisa Owings.
Description: Minneapolis, MN : Bellwether Media Inc., 2017. | Series: Epic:
   Ghost Stories | Includes bibliographical references and index.
Identifiers: LCCN 2015049953 | ISBN 9781626174320 (hardcover : alk. paper)
Subjects: LCSH: Ghosts–Washington (D.C.)–Juvenile literature. | White House
   (Washington, D.C.)–Juvenile literature. | Haunted houses–Washington
   (D.C.)–Juvenile literature.
Classification: LCC BF1472.U6 O95 2017 | DDC 133.1/29753–dc23
LC record available at http://lccn.loc.gov/2015049953

Printed in the United States of America, North Mankato, MN.

TABLE OF CONTENTS

HAUNTINGS

You are a guest at the White House in Washington, D.C. Friends swear it is haunted. They have told stories of White House ghosts.

As you slip into bed, someone knocks on your door. You answer it. But no one is in sight!

THE PHANTOM PRESIDENT

Abraham Lincoln was president in the 1860s. He was **assassinated** in 1865. But he may have unfinished business in the White House.

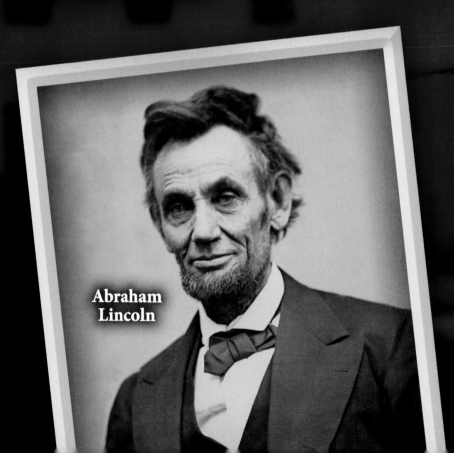

Abraham
Lincoln

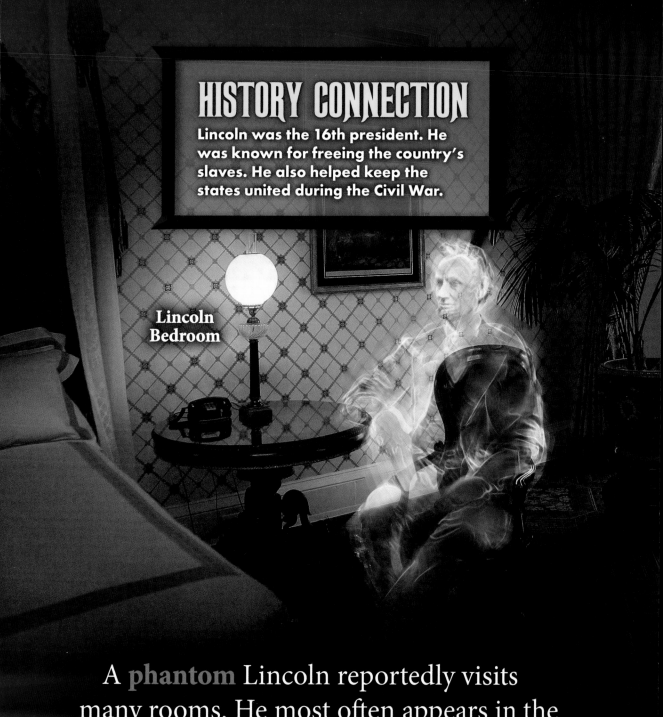

Lincoln Bedroom

A **phantom** Lincoln reportedly visits many rooms. He most often appears in the Lincoln Bedroom.

People hear Lincoln's footsteps.
Sometimes his ghost knocks on doors.

SPIRIT SNAPSHOT

A photo of Lincoln's wife, Mary, shows his ghost behind her. Many people think the photo is fake. But Mary believed in the spirit world.

In 1942, the Queen of the Netherlands stayed at the White House. She answered a knock late one night. There was Lincoln's ghost, wearing a **top hat**. She fainted!

Queen Wilhelmina
of the Netherlands

British leader Winston Churchill also met Lincoln's ghost. Churchill was walking from the bath to his room. He came face-to-face with the former president.

Churchill avoided the bedroom after that. Would you be brave enough to sleep there?

SIGHTINGS OF ABRAHAM LINCOLN

- Appears in portrait of Lincoln's wife (1870s)

- Stands before First Lady Grace Coolidge in the Oval Office (1920s)

- Surprises Winston Churchill in his bedroom (1940s)

- Appears at the door of Queen Wilhelmina of the Netherlands (1942)

- Scares maid while pulling on boots (1930s–40s)

- Appears to Ronald Reagan's daughter at night (1980s)

ALL GEARED UP

Lincoln's ghost gave Eleanor
Roosevelt's maid a fright.
She saw him on a bed,
putting on boots. She
ran from the room!

ABIGAIL'S AFTERLIFE

Abigail Adams was married to John Adams. He was the second president of the United States.

They were the first couple to live in the White House. But Abigail's spirit may still **linger**.

John Adams

Abigail Adams

HISTORY CONNECTION

Abigail Adams was interested in politics. Women had few rights back then. She fought for their right to education.

13

In Adams' time, much of the White House was damp and chilly. So she hung her laundry in the warm, dry East Room.

Now her ghost rushes to that room in a cap and **shawl**. It looks as if she is carrying wash.

EAST ROOM HAUNTS

Lincoln's ghost has also been spotted in the East Room. It is where his body lay after his death.

Staff says the East Room sometimes smells of fresh laundry. But no one hangs clothes there anymore.

East Room

SIGHTINGS OF ABIGAIL ADAMS
- Floated through doors in front of President Taft and others (early 1900s)
- Spotted by several visitors (2002)

Lincoln and Adams are just two White House ghosts. Many others are said to haunt the halls!

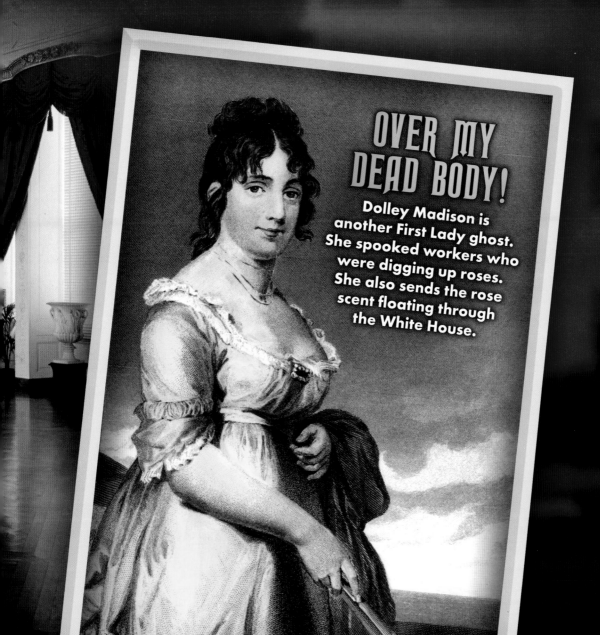

OVER MY DEAD BODY!

Dolley Madison is another First Lady ghost. She spooked workers who were digging up roses. She also sends the rose scent floating through the White House.

WAKING DREAMS OR WHITE HOUSE GHOSTS?

Many White House ghost sightings happen at night. Skeptics say these are hallucinations.

They often happen between wake and sleep. Ghostly visions are common in this dreamy state.

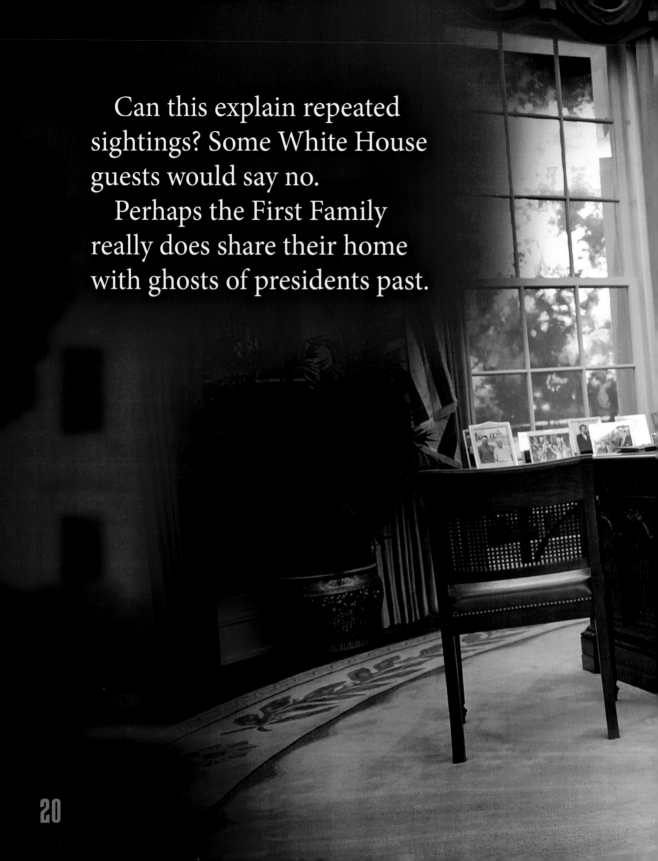

Can this explain repeated sightings? Some White House guests would say no.

Perhaps the First Family really does share their home with ghosts of presidents past.

21

GLOSSARY

assassinated—killed for political reasons

hallucinations—things that people see or hear but that are not there

linger—to remain

phantom—ghostly

shawl—a piece of cloth worn to cover the shoulders or head

skeptics—people who doubt the truth of something

top hat—a tall, black dress hat

visions—things that are dreamed or seen in the mind

TO LEARN MORE

AT THE LIBRARY

Anderson, AnnMarie. *When I Grow Up: Abraham Lincoln.* New York, N.Y.: Scholastic Inc., 2015.

Higgins, Nadia. *Ghosts.* Minneapolis, Minn.: Bellwether Media, 2014.

Rajczak, Michael. *Haunted! The White House.* New York, N.Y.: Gareth Stevens Publishing, 2014.

ON THE WEB

Learning more about ghosts in the White House is as easy as 1, 2, 3.

1. Go to www.factsurfer.com.

2. Enter "ghosts in the White House" into the search box.

3. Click the "Surf" button and you will see a list of related web sites.

With factsurfer.com, finding more information is just a click away.

INDEX